I'm No Scaredy Cat …

But I'm Afraid to Go to School!

Author: Angela Cleveland

Illustrator: Beth Pierce

Confident Counselor Publishing

Angela Cleveland

Copyright © 2018 by Angela Cleveland. All rights reserved.

Published by Confident Counselor
13 Tanglewood Court,
Monmouth Junction, NJ 08852

TABLE OF CONTENTS

DEDICATION

This book is dedicated to children who struggle with worried feelings and families and friends who love them.

ACKNOWLEDGEMENTS

I would like to express my gratitude to my mentors and colleagues. As a school counselor, I am blessed to work with a wonderful group of educators who serve as a support system for our students. They foster a positive school climate where all children feel accepted, respected, and heard. They are a daily inspiration to me and role models to our students.

I am grateful for the support of friend and former colleague Marianne Lawless. Her honest and wise feedback as both my editor and fellow educator helped to shape this story.

CHAPTER 1:

THE BUS STOP

Sydney had a strange, nervous feeling fluttering around her tummy. Her heart was beating quickly and a horrible, terrible feeling came over her. Just thinking of going to school that morning filled her body with fear. This was such a confusing feeling for Sydney because she loved school! Her teacher, Ms. Pawsome, was fun and friendly. Her best friends, Smokey, Belle, and Mags, would be expecting her.

"Are you okay, Sydney?" Papa asked. He felt Sydney's forehead to see if she had a fever. "You haven't eaten any breakfast." A bowl of sardines sat untouched in front of Sydney.

"I don't feel well," whispered Sydney. "Can I stay home with you?" Papa stroked Sydney's fur, looked in her ears, and rubbed her cheeks.

"You don't seem sick. You are just kitten me." Papa said with a smile. He hoped to lighten her mood with a little joke. When he saw that she was not smiling back he looked deeply into her soft green eyes and asked, "What's wrong?"

"I don't know," whispered Sydney. "I'm not kidding. I really don't want to go to school."

"Aren't you starting to plan for the annual science fair?" Mama asked as she walked in the kitchen. The fourth graders at Cat Mountain Elementary School looked forward to the science fair, a special celebration where they shared their projects. The students were allowed to pick any topic they were curious about. They researched it and conducted an experiment. They presented their results to their teachers, families, and all of the other elementary school students at the annual science fair.

"What experiment are you planning?" Mama asked.

Looking down at her paws, Sydney whispered, "I am going to do an experiment to see if all cats really do like catnip."

Rupert, Sydney's little brother scampered into the kitchen. "Are we talking about catnip? Can I have some? Where is it?" Rupert's whiskers twitched in excitement.

"We're talking about Sydney's science experiment," Mama explained to Rupert. She turned back to Sydney and asked, "How is your experiment going to work?"

Sydney's eyes remained focused on her paws as she answered. "I'm going to give cats some spinach and some catnip. I won't tell them which one they are eating. Then I ask them which one they liked more.

"That sounds like a great experiment," Mama said with pride. "I can't wait to see the results!"

Rupert's tail flicked side to side in excitement "Can I have the leftover catnip?" he begged.

"We'll see about that," answered Mama. She slipped on her favorite purple pearl necklace and leaned over to kiss Sydney on the forehead.

"Well," Papa said as he patted Sydney on the head, "If you aren't sick, you have to go to school." Mama nodded in agreement.

Mama leaned over Sydney to kiss Papa. She scratched Sydney behind her ears and then ruffled the fur on top of Rupert's head. Mama picked up her laptop bag and sang, "Have a claw-some day!" as she left for work at Tabby Technology Company.

Papa helped Sydney and Rupert put on their backpacks, tucking Mousey safely inside Rupert's backpack for show-and-tell that day.

"But I don't want to go to school," Sydney repeated, dragging her paws as Papa walked her and Rupert outside to the bus stop.

"I know," said Papa, "but you'll feel better once you get on the bus." Sydney *did not* think she would feel better.

As Papa walked them to the bus stop, Rupert chatted about what he was going to tell the class about Mousey, but Sydney did not talk at all. The horrible, terrible feeling got worse with each step. The fluttering feeling in her tummy now felt like angry buzzing bees. Her paws felt cold and hot all at once. Her heart felt like it was beating, beating, beating against her chest like it was trying to escape. Even her heart didn't want to go to school!

The horrible, terrible feeling washed over Sydney, as she watched the big, yellow school bus slow to a stop. The bus door swung open. The driver, Mr. Pounce, waved hello to Papa, Sydney, and Rupert. With each step Sydney took to board the bus ahead of her, she felt the horrible, terrible feeling increasing. It made her paws feel so heavy that she could barely lift them to climb the bus stairs.

Sydney suddenly turned away from the bus, ran to Papa, and she wrapped all four of her silver-tipped paws around Papa. Tears filled her eyes, slid down her whiskers, and fell to the ground. Papa was surprised and worried about his fur-baby. Sydney had never done anything like this before.

"Sydney, sweetie, what's going on?" Papa asked as he stroked Sydney's ears. Sydney was crying so very hard that she could not speak. She gulped for air and her shoulders shook as she sobbed. Even if she could speak, she did not have the words to explain this horrible, terrible feeling.

"Is everything okay, Mr. Lion?" asked Mr. Pounce as he leaned over the giant steering wheel and frowned with concern at Sydney.

"I don't know," Papa replied. "Why don't you just go ahead, and I can bring Sydney to school myself." Mr.

Pounce slowly nodded with a concerned frown, and he waved goodbye to Papa.

The bus door swung closed. Papa looked up to see Rupert's nose and paw pressed against the bus window. "It's going to be okay!" Papa called out to Rupert. Rupert smiled weakly back at Papa. What was wrong with Sydney?

CHAPTER 2:

A BAD FEELING

Papa carried Sydney home. She cried and cried the whole way back to the house. Papa stroked her golden fur. "It's okay," he reassured her. "It's okay." Papa was worried. He laid Sydney down on the couch and got her a bowl of cold water. He sat next to her and scratched her chin, cheeks, and just behind her ears. Papa knew just what to do to help Sydney relax, and before long, Sydney stopped sobbing and began purring.

"Sydney," Papa asked, "please tell me what's going on." He handed her the bowl of water.

Sydney took a long drink of water and then looked into Papa's eyes.

"I don't know," she said. "I have a horrible, terrible feeling." Sydney thought about how she felt, but it was hard to describe. "I feel like something bad is going to happen."

"Bad?" Papa asked. "To you? Is something happening at school?"

Sydney frowned and thought about the feeling. "Everything is great at school. I don't know why I feel like this." Sydney shook her head and looked down. She felt embarrassed, confused, and sad. She felt so very, very sad. She was no scaredy cat, so why was she so afraid to go to school?

"Well," said Papa, thinking hard about what to do, "I'm going to give the school counselor a call and see if she can help us figure this out."

"Ms. Meow?" Sydney asked. She had never really spoken to Ms. Meow except when she visited their classroom to teach lessons about friendship, study skills, and about having a paws-i-tive cat-i-tude.

"Yes," replied Papa as he patted Sydney on the head and stood to get the phone. Papa punched Cat Mountain Elementary School's number into his phone and selected the option to speak to Ms. Meow.

"Hello," answered Ms. Meow, "this is the school counselor. How can I help you?"

"Hello," replied Papa, "this is Mr. Lion, Sydney's dad. I have Sydney here with me. She is having a tough morning." Sydney's ears twitched with nervousness as she listened to Papa's side of the conversation. Would she be in trouble for not going to school? What if Ms. Meow said she had to go to class? Sydney felt scared. The horrible, terrible feeling churned in her belly.

"Oh yes, Mr. Lion. I noticed Sydney is absent today," Ms. Meow said. "We're in period two, we were worried since it's rare for Sydney to miss school. How is she doing?"

"Well," Papa began, "I'm not sure. You see, Sydney doesn't seem sick. She doesn't have a fever, stuffy nose, or cough, yet she does not want to go to school."

"Hmmm," Ms. Meow said, "Did she say if anything is bothering her at school?"

"No," Papa replied. "Sydney has friends, she likes her teacher, and she is not having any trouble with her claws-work. Still, she does not want to go to school."

"I see," replied Ms. Meow. "It must be very confusing for Sydney and for you. Let's work together as a team to understand what is happening and help Sydney feel comfortable. Can you come to school this morning with Sydney? That way the three of us can talk more about how she is feeling?"

"Yes," Papa replied, "We can come in now." When Sydney heard that, tears filled her eyes again. The tears splashed left and right as she shook her head no. She just could not go to school.

Papa saw how upset Sydney was and said, "Uh, Ms. Meow, Sydney feels strongly about *not* coming into school. It might be tough."

"I understand," said Ms. Meow soothingly. "Please let Sydney know that she does not have to go to her classes today, but it is very important that she comes to school. She can stay with me in my office. The most important thing is that she comes to school. The longer she waits, the harder it can get."

"Okay," Papa said to Ms. Meow while looking at Sydney, "so she does not have to go to any classes when we come to school this morning, right?" When Sydney heard this, she picked her head up and looked at Papa. She didn't want to go to school, but what was this about not having to go to classes?

"Yes," said Ms. Meow firmly. "Please bring Sydney in so we can talk more about what's going on. She will not have to go to any classes today unless she wants to."

"Alrighty then," Papa sighed. "I will let Sydney know that we are going to meet and that she does not have to go to class today." He smiled at Sydney and added, "Fur real." Sydney didn't grin at Papa's joke like she usually did. "We'll see you soon."

Papa hung up the phone, and sat down next to Sydney on the couch. "Well, what do you think, sweetie? Ms. Meow said you won't have to go to class today, but she does want us to come to school and see her."

"I don't want to go to school," Sydney mumbled.

"I know you don't," Papa said. "I'm going to be right there with you, and we are just going to talk to Ms. Meow." Papa stroked Sydney's chin and scratched behind her ears. Sydney breathing had slowed and she felt a little better. She thought about meeting with Ms. Meow. She seemed nice.

"Maybe Ms. Meow can help meow-t?" Sydney whispered as she slid her eyes toward Papa's to see if he caught her joke.

"Thank you, sweetie," Papa said while patting Sydney on the head. "I know this isn't easy. It takes a lot of courage."

Papa then pressed his forehead to Sydney's and added.
"I'm litter-ally very proud of you for being willing to try."

CHAPTER 3:

MEETING WITH MS. MEOW

Papa parked his car in the visitor spot at Cat Mountain Elementary School. He looked in the rearview mirror at Sydney sitting in the back seat with her head down. He sighed deeply and stepped out of the car. He opened the car door and unbuckled Sydney's seat belt.

"I don't want to go to school," she whispered. "I'm scared." The horrible, terrible feeling whirled around in her tummy. Her arms felt heavy. Her paws felt like she was wearing heavy boots and gloves.

"It's going to be okay," Papa said with a smile. He reached out with his big silver paw. Sydney just stared at it. She shook her head no.

"I promise, I'll stay with you the whole time and all day if you need me to. You're not doing this alone. I'm right here with you." He continued to hold his paw out to Sydney.

She took a deep breath and looked up at Papa. Sydney put her little silver paw in his. She slowly, slowly, slowly walked with Papa into Cat Mountain Elementary School.

"Pardon me. We are here to see Ms. Meow," Papa said to the secretary in the main office.

"Sure thing, Mr. Lion," she chirped. "She is expecting you. I'll walk you to her office." She guided Mr. Lion and Sydney to a colorful office filled with books, little squeeze toys, and other interesting items.

"Sydney! I'm so happy to see you!" exclaimed Ms. Meow. "Mr. Lion, welcome," she added as she extended a paw to him. "It looks like we have had quite a tough morning. Come, please sit," Ms. Meow said pointing to a dark wooden round table with four chairs around it.

Once everyone found a seat, Ms. Meow leaned toward Sydney and asked, "Sydney, whatever is going on, however you are feeling, please know that you are not alone. Your fur-family and I are here to help you. Can you tell me a little about what's happening?"

Sydney nodded and took a deep breath. She wanted to tell Ms. Meow, but how could she explain this horrible, terrible feeling? "I-, I-, um-, I don't know. I'm just scared. I think."

"It takes a brave cat to talk about such a hard thing, Sydney," Ms. Meow said patting Sydney's paw. "Can you tell me more about when this feeling started?"

"I think this morning," Sydney said as she thought hard. "I just felt scared, like something bad was going to happen. I mean, nothing is bad at school or at home. So, I don't know..."

"Can you explain more about how your body felt this morning?"

"My paws felt sweaty and cold," Sydney recalled. "My tummy hurt. My heart was beating really, really hard." As she spoke, Sydney could feel herself breathing faster. "I thought that something bad would happen in class, like I would be sick. I wanted to stay with Papa."

"That does sound like a bad feeling," Ms. Meow nodded. "I can understand why you would want to stay home. Do you remember what you were thinking about when you had these feelings?"

Sydney scratched her head. "Hmmm. I was thinking about a lot of things. I was thinking about the science fair and I was scared that I might mess up my project." Ms. Meow nodded encouragingly to Sydney. "I was thinking about the big leaves in the yard, and I wondered what would happen if I got lost inside the big pile and nobody ever found me."

Sydney scratched her head again. "I was scared that I might come home from school and not know where Papa is. Most days he is home, but some days he goes to the office." Tears filled Sydney's eyes.

Papa scratched the spot just behind Sydney's ears and kissed the top of her head. Sydney said, "I feel like I have a scary worry monster living in my head!"

Ms. Meow nodded and patted Sydney's paw again. "I know you're scared, and those certainly are some frightening thoughts. I have a few things we can do right now to help tame that worry monster."

"Do I have to go to class?" Sydney asked with wide, scared eyes.

"Let's take it one day at a time," Ms. Meow smiled. "Right now, you are here with your Papa and me. Nobody is talking about you going to class, right?" Sydney nodded and relaxed just a little bit.

"Okay," Sydney said. She was curious about what Ms. Meow could do to help her.

CHAPTER 4:

LEARNING SOMETHING NEW

Ms. Meow said. "We all feel worried about things from time to time. It's completely normal. I'll share with you something that really helps me and many other cats when we have this feeling. Are you ready?" Sydney nodded. "Mr. Lion, you can join us in this activity. It's called 'visualization.' It means we are going to picture things in our heads." Papa nodded and settled comfortably into his chair.

"First, let's take our shoulders and roll them back in five BIG circles." Ms. Meow demonstrated. Papa and Sydney followed along. "Now let's roll our shoulders forward in five BIG circles." Ms. Meow demonstrated. Papa and Sydney followed along. "Find a comfortable way to sit and close your eyes." Ms. Meow moved her head a little from side-to-side, dropped her shoulders and closed her eyes. Papa and Sydney followed along.

"I want you to think of a real place, someplace familiar where you have been where you felt safe, relaxed, and happy. It could be a place outside surrounded by nature. It could be a cozy place inside in your home where you feel your best. The place could be anywhere you choose. The most important thing is that you pick a place where you feel safe, relaxed, and happy. I'm going to give you a few moments to pull that place to mind."

Sydney thought about her family and her friends. She thought about school and playing outside at recess. Where was a place she felt happiest? Suddenly, an image bright as the sun filled her head!

"When you have your place in mind," Ms. Meow softly said, "Use all of your senses to remember everything about this place. Think of the colors, the sounds, the smells, and how the place looks and feels."

Sydney closed her eyes and thought about playing with Rupert in the bright, green mountain grass. She smiled thinking of how the grass tickled her back as she rolled in it. She could smell the fresh shoots and hear how the leaves in the trees rustled and swayed in the mountain breezes. She smell the honeysuckle and could taste the sweet nectar she licked from the flower. Sydney felt a smile lift her cheeks and felt the tension ease from her shoulders. The butterflies in her tummy fluttered far away and a warm rush of peaceful calm took their place.

"Let's take some deeeeeep breaths together," Ms. Meow said softly. "Imagine you have a balloon in your belly. We are going to take such big breaths that we fill that balloon up." Ms. Meow slowly counted to five, and Sydney and Papa followed along.

"Slowly breathe in. One… two… three… four… five. Slowly breathe out. Five… four… three… two… one." Ms. Meow repeated the breathing activity several more times while Sydney and Papa pictured in their heads filling the imaginary balloon in their bellies.

Sydney placed her paw over her belly and felt it swell with refreshing air as she breathed in. She imagined all the scary and bad feelings leaving her belly with each slow whoosh of breath she let out.

"Continue to take the deep breaths and keep thinking about your special place." Ms. Meow said softly, "We are going to practice tensing and relaxing our muscles. Let's start with the very tips of our paws. Squeeze all the muscles there, hold, and relax."

Sydney and Papa thought about all the muscles in their paws as they squeezed, held them for a moment, and then relaxed them. Ms. Meow instructed Sydney and Papa to squeeze and relax their muscles moving from the tips of their paws to the tips of their ears. Once they finished, Ms. Meow said, "Now slowly open your eyes." Papa and Sydney's eyes fluttered open.

"How do you feel?" Ms. Meow asked.

Sydney smiled at Papa and said, "I'm feline better. I liked that!"

Papa winked at Sydney in agreement, "She must be feeling better."

"I definitely feel more relaxed," said Sydney.

"Wonderful!" Ms. Meow said. "You can do this at home, before school, or even come back here to see me if you are feeling it might help you manage your day."

Sydney smiled and took a deep, slow breath. She felt relaxed, but she still did not want to go to class. What if the horrible, terrible feeling came back? "Do I have to go to class now?" she whispered.

Ms. Meow glanced at the clock and said, "Well, lunchtime and recess are starting in just a few minutes. How do you feel about starting your day with some fresh sardines and warm milk? That's the special today! What do you think? Are you up to it?"

Sydney LOVED sardine and warm milk day, but she hesitated, "What if the horrible, terrible feeling comes back?"

"If it does, you can always come back to see me. I'm here for you. Some cats find that it helps to take a quick walk to the water bowl, to visit the litter box, or to take a moment to walk in the hallways, look at the bulletin boards, and then return to class. You can try that, too."

Sydney thought about what the afternoon might feel like.

"And remember," Ms. Meow said, "You can always come back and see me. You don't have to stay in class today, but if you do, I'll check up on you this afternoon to see how you are feeling."

Sydney smiled and said, "Okay, I think...I think I'll try."

"We can talk more at home and try some of Ms. Meow's exercises," Papa said as he rubbed Sydney's head, just behind her silver-tipped ears.

Just then, the bell rang. The bells at Cat Mountain Elementary School sounded like happy meows rather than an actual bell. Sydney hugged Papa and smiled at Ms. Meow. "I'm a little nervous about going to the cafeteria. Can you walk me there, Ms. Meow?"

"Certainly!" She replied. "I'll help you find Mags, Belle, and Smokey and get settled in."

CHAPTER 5:

PRACTICE MAKES PERMANENT

Sydney watched Papa prepare dinner for the family. It had been a long day, and she looked forward to dinner. Sydney's ears twitched when Papa opened the yellow kitchen cabinets, removed a can of Feast of Fish cat food, and held the can under the automatic humming can opener. Sydney purred loudly in anticipation of the yummy meal to come.

When Papa met Sydney and Rupert at the bus stop, Papa asked her about her day. Sydney explained that she "paw-furred" to first write down some ideas and talk about it over dinner. She was looking forward to a yummy meal and talking to Mama, Papa, and Rupert.

"Wash your paws," Mama gently reminded Sydney and Rupert. Immediately the siblings licked their paws, but they never took their eyes off Papa. He was an expert scooper, and he carefully scooped Feast of Fish into four yellow bowls. The mouthwatering scent of sardines, salmon, and shrimp filled the kitchen. Papa brought the bowls to the kitchen table and placed one heaping bowl in front of Rupert, one heaping bowl in front of Sydney, one heaping bowl in front of Mama, and one heaping bowl in front of his seat at the table. Papa sat down to join the rest of the family for dinner.

"Let's eat!" Papa announced. Mama, Papa, Sydney, and Rupert leaned into their bowls and began dining on Feast of Fish.

"So," Sydney began, "The afternoon was okay, but I thought the horrible, terrible feeling was coming back during hiss-tory class. I took a walk to the water bowl, like Ms. Meow said to do, and I felt better. Ms. Meow checked in on me at the end of the day and gave me this "Courageous Cat" smelly sticker."

Sydney rubbed the pink sticker on her paw, and the smell of tuna and chicken filled the air. "I'm worried about the feeling coming back though."

"We're here for you, Sydney," Mama said. "You aren't alone in this. We can do the exercises that Ms. Meow taught you together as a family."

"That's right," agreed Papa. "The more we practice, the better we'll all be at managing all of our worried feelings. Practice will help make the calm feeling more permanent and lasting."

"Do you have worried feelings, too?" Sydney asked Papa.

"Of course!" he replied. "Everyone has worried feelings from time to time. Do you want to know my trick for managing them?" Sydney nodded her head. She was one curious cat!

"I use music. I have a playlist of my favorite songs that make me feel strong, confident, and powerful. I call it "Papa's Paw-erful Playlist." I listen to the songs on my playlist when I need a mood boost or when I'm having a tough time. I can share my songs with you, and we can make a paw-erful playlist for you, if you like."

Sydney nodded her head excitedly. She thought about playing the songs in the morning before school, on the bus while using her earbuds, or even at recess time.

Sydney turned to Mama and asked, "Do you ever have worried feelings?"

"Of course!" Mama replied. "When I do, I think about someone I admire very much." Mama rubbed Sydney's ears and asked her, "You know that Papa picked your first name, but I picked your middle name. Did I ever tell you why I picked "Amelia" to be your middle name?"

Sydney shook her head no. She remembered Papa telling her about the amazing opera house in Sydney, Australia, which was the inspiration for her first name. But, she never knew why "Amelia" was her middle name.

"I picked the name Amelia for you because I greatly admire the famous pilot, Amelia Earhart. I often think about how much courage it took for her to be the first female aviator to fly alone across the Atlantic Ocean. It was a long time ago. Airplanes were still very new. On top of that, there were not many female pilots. Amelia had to find her inner courage and strength to accomplish her dreams. She blocked out the negative voices in her mind and from critical cats who told her she couldn't and shouldn't fly an airplane. When I feel like I can't do something, or that it's too hard to even try, I think about Amelia Earhart. I imagine her cheering me on and telling me that I can do it."

"Wow," breathed Sydney. She never knew about Amelia Earhart, and she felt excited to learn more.

"Do you want to know what I do when I have worried feelings?," asked Rupert softly. Mama, Papa, and Sydney turned to Rupert, all nodding their heads. "I hug Mousey," he said, holding out his favorite stuffed animal and placing it on Sydney's lap. "You can borrow him for hugs whenever you need to."

"Thanks," Sydney said with a big grin. She hugged Mousey tightly and smiled at Rupert, Mama, and Papa.

"Ms. Meow gave me a special notebook at the end of the day. She called it a journal and explained that it can be really helpful to write down my worries or even draw pictures. Ms. Meow said that it helps to get the scary thoughts out of my head. I can use the journal to remind myself of how I learned to manage my feelings."

"What a wonderful idea," Mama said with a big smile. Sydney took a deep breath and smiled at Mama, Papa, and Rupert. Knowing she had her family, friends, teachers, and school counselor there to support her would help chase the worry monster away.

CHAPTER 6:

A PAGE FROM SYDNEY'S JOURNAL

It's been about two months since I started writing. It helps to get my feelings out on paper. Sometimes I write and sometimes I draw pictures. It all depends on my mood. I like keeping track of when I feel the terrible feeling and what helps me to feel better. I like the deep breathing, muscle relaxation, and picturing my special place when the terrible feeling is at its worst.

Ms. Meow helped me to list all the things I can do if the horrible, terrible feeling comes back. We wrote all of our ideas down on a little index card. It helps me because sometimes I forget what to do when the feeling starts.

With Papa's help, I created " Sydney's Paw-erful Playlist." I listen to my favorite meow-sicians every morning. Actually, Mama, Papa, Rupert and I all made our own "Paw-erful Playlists." We love sharing songs with each other.

Mama bought me a special "good luck charm" to wear on my collar. It's a little metal circle with a picture of Cat Mountain on it. Mama told me that a mountain can feel impossible to climb, but simply focus on putting one paw in front of the other. Before you know it, you will be on top of the mountain!

My friend Smokey told me that he writes in a journal every single day and how it helps him to get his purr-sonal feelings out. He said that he really enjoys the quiet time to think about things, and he always feels better afterward.

One of the things I've been thinking about is how Amelia is my middle name, and I like to think that I have some of Amelia Earhart's courage and strength inside of me. It's a nice thought!

Well, that's about it for today! It's snowing! I can't wait to go outside with Rupert, have a big snowball fight and build snow-cats. Once our noses turn from pink to bright red, Mama always calls us inside. She takes a warm towel from the dryer to wipe the cold snowflakes from our fur. Papa gives us warm milk and we relax on the rug in front of the glowing fireplace. Hmmm, I think I have a new special place for me to think about!

Sydney

CHAPTER 7:

STRESS LESS

Try some of Ms. Meow's and Sydney Lion's favorite de-stressors:

Talk it out!

Talk to a trusted adult, friend, or even a pet. It can be really hard to talk about tough stuff, but it's even harder to hold it all in. Sometimes others can help you brainstorm solutions you hadn't considered. Mostly, it feels really good to just talk about it. Some people say it's easier to talk while doing another activity, like playing a board game, shooting hoops, or taking a walk. What's your talking style?

Keep a Journal

Sydney and her friend Smokey recommend keeping a journal to get all of your thoughts out on paper. They like re-reading what they wrote or drew pictures of and thinking about how they managed difficult situations and their feelings. You can write down your worried feelings or draw pictures in a special notebook or journal.

Visualization

Do you remember when Ms. Meow talked about visualizing a happy place? Did you know that during that time, both Papa and Ms. Meow thought of their happy places.

Papa thought about the family kitchen. He loved preparing dinner each night. There was a moment each evening before he placed dinner on the table when he looked at his family and felt a sense of gratitude wash over him. He felt like the most fortunate cat in the world, and he always took time to let that feeling sink in.

Ms. Meow thought about Cat Creek, the clear mountain stream that brought fresh water from the top of Cat Mountain to the valley below. She loved dipping her paws in the cold water on a hot summer day while she lay in the bright green grass reading a good book. The sun would warm her orange fur, the grass would tickle her ears as she relaxed in it, and the cold Cat Creek water would be refreshing and relaxing as she listened to it lazily roll over brown and gray stones in the creek.

Picture in your head a calm, relaxing, safe place. Use all of your five senses to bring the place to mind:

- Hearing – What does your special place sound like? What are the big sounds you first notice and the quieter sounds in the distance?

- Smelling – What lovely smells can you find in your special place? Do you smell chicken noodle soup boiling on a stove or the crisp, crunchy autumn leaves?

- Seeing – What are the big and small details in your special place? Picture every small object from the single grain of sand, blade of grass, or other tiny detail.

- Touching – What do the things in your special place feel like? What are the unique textures you experience as you run your hands over them?

- Tasting – What tastes touch your tongue? It could be a real taste of food you've eaten or an imagined taste of salty ocean water or sweet honeysuckle.

Deep Breathing

Try some deep belly breathing. Imagine you have a balloon in your belly that you are going to fill up. Place your hand over your belly button to be sure you are filling up the balloon. You will know when you doing just that because your hand will naturally rise and fall with your breaths. Breathe in to the slow count of five. Hold. Breathe out to the slow count of five. Repeat five times (or more for even more relaxation benefits). This is a simple exercise you can do while lying in bed if you are having trouble sleeping. You can also practice deep belly breathing in school or on the school bus!

Muscle Relaxation

Working from your toes to the tippy top of your head, squeeze, hold, and then relax all of your muscles. Focus on just one muscle group at a time. This is an excellent way to relax your body before you fall asleep, but you can use it during the day, too. Sometimes, when we are stressed, we squeeze our muscles really tightly. This activity helps you to relax the muscles you may not even know you are keeping really tense and tight.

Comfort Item

Find or make a special charm that reminds you of how strong you are. Sydney loves her Cat Mountain charm, and she is saving her allowance to buy an airplane charm that will be a reminder of Amelia Earhart's courage (which is a real inspiration to Sydney). What is something you can wear or carry with you that will remind you of your inner strength? In your special notebook, draw a picture of what your charm would look like.

Playlist

Create a "Powerful Playlist" of your favorite tunes that make you feel strong and confident. Play the songs while you are getting ready for school, on your way to school, or any time you need a quick mood boost.

Look to a Role Model

Identifying a role model you admire can help you focus on your goals, especially during hard times. Mama and Sydney admire Amelia Earhart's courage and strength. Your role model can be someone you know personally or someone you have read about. They can be living now or someone who was once living. Who is your role model? What qualities does that person have that you admire? Draw a picture or write about your role model in your special notebook.

Keep a List

Ms. Meow recommends writing down a list of things you can do to tame the worry monster. Sometimes, when we are going through a difficult time, it helps to look at your list and know that you have several things you can do, caring adults and friends you can talk to, and that you are not alone. Below is a picture of what Sydney's list looks like. In your special notebook, make a list of people you can talk to and things you can do if you feel worried or have stressful feelings.

If I feel the horrible, terrible feeling, I can:

1. Talk to an adult (family, teacher, counselor) or a friend.
2. Take a break (get a drink of water or use the litter box).
3. Take some deep breaths and relax my muscles.
4. In my mind, picture my happy place.
5. Listen to my Paw-erful Playlist of songs.
6. Hug Mousey.
7. Think of Amelia Earhart.
8. Write or draw in my journal.
9. Know that even if the feeling comes back, it won't last ever.
10. Know that I'm not alone.

CHAPTER 8:

PUNNY STUFF

I'm No Scaredy Cat … But I'm Afraid to Go to School! contains many puns. Puns are jokes that play with the sounds and meanings of words. For some people going through a tough time, laughter is the best medicine.

Below are some examples of puns from this story:

- "You don't seem sick. You are just kitten me." (kidding)
- "She had never really spoken to Ms. Meow except when she visited their classroom to teach lessons about friendship, study skills, and about having a paws-i-tive cat-i-tude." (positive attitude)
- "Maybe Ms. Meow can help meow-t?" (me out)

That's some punny stuff! Can you find the puns in these sentences?

- "Sydney has friends, likes her teacher, and she is not having any trouble with her claws-work."
- "He smiled at Sydney and added, 'Fur real.'"
- "Sydney smiled at Papa and said, "I'm feline better."
- "The afternoon was okay, but I thought the horrible, terrible feeling was coming back during hiss-tory class."
- "I can share my songs with you, and we can make a paw-erful playlist for you, if you like."
- "I listen to my favorite meow-sicians every morning."
- "My friend Smokey told me that he writes in a journal every single day and how it helps him to get his purr-sonal feelings out."

CHAPTER 9:

WORD SEARCH

```
C C A M E L I A E A R H A R T M A U
O V L A N R U O J O V F A M I L Y A
U S D M G N I H T A E R B P E E D L
N T B R O L E M O D E L G B V A Q J
S P U N J B U C A T M O U N T A I N
E C A L P Y P P A H P Q X A M A M P
L W O R R Y M O N S T E R J T R O I
O A M S M E O W C O M F O R T C B N
R P O Y B S W A P R U O Y H S A W T
W A W R S Y D N E Y J P K O V Y R A
L P H S I F F O T S A E F Y N D K C
R U P E R T M D P L A Y L I S T P J
```

AMELIA EARHART	DEEP BREATHING	MAMA	ROLE MODEL
CAT MOUNTAIN	FAMILY	MS MEOW	RUPERT
CATNIP	FEAST OF FISH	PAPA	SYDNEY
COMFORT	HAPPY PLACE	PLAYLIST	WASH YOUR PAWS
COUNSELOR	JOURNAL	PUN	WORRY MONSTER

AUTHOR'S NOTE

Everyone experiences feelings of worry on occasion. Those diagnosed with Generalized Anxiety Disorder worry excessively about many areas of their life (ex: work/school, friends, family, etc...). They worry that their worst possible fears will happen. They experience many physical symptoms as a result of their anxiety (headaches, stomach pains, heart racing, etc...), and these symptoms are often so severe that it significantly impacts their ability to attend work/school and even participate in fun social events.

To learn more about GAD (Generalized Anxiety Disorder), visit the <u>National Institute of Mental Health</u>. Reach out to a medical professional for assistance. There are many treatment options available, and people struggling with GAD can find support and help.

If you or someone you love is having a difficult time, talk to a trusted adult. Many people find it's helpful to talk to a school counselor or a counselor outside of school. You can also call 1-800-273-TALK (8255) to speak to someone anonymously and free of charge anytime of the day or night.

ABOUT THE AUTHOR

With 15 years of experience as a professional school counselor, Angela Cleveland has enjoyed working with a diverse population of students. Angela is a contributor to national publications, such as Edutopia, CSTA Voice, and ASCA's School Counselor magazine.

Angela's advocacy has earned her professional recognition, such as the NJ "2017 NJ State School Counselor of the Year."

Angela co-founded ReigningIt (www.ReigningIt.com), "creating a #STEM dialogue inclusive of every woman."

Learn more about Angela. Follow her on Twitter (@AngCleveland) and visit: www.AngelaCleveland.com.

ABOUT THE ILLUSTRATOR

Beth Pierce is an office worker by day, freelance cartoonist by night. She lives in New Jersey with her husband, daughter and two crazy cats.

Beth's artwork can be found on Instagram (instagram.com/littlebchan) and Tumblr (littlebchan.tumblr.com).

Made in the USA
Lexington, KY
28 May 2018